# Out of This World:

## The Surreal Art of Leonora Carrington

Written by Michelle Markel      Illustrated by Amanda Hall

**BALZER + BRAY**
*An Imprint of HarperCollinsPublishers*

Balzer + Bray is an imprint of HarperCollins Publishers.

Out of This World: The Surreal Art of Leonora Carrington
Text copyright © 2019 by Michelle Markel
Illustrations copyright © 2019 by Amanda Hall
All rights reserved. Manufactured in China.

ISBN 978-0-06-244109-6

Typography by Dana Fritts
The artist used watercolor inks and gouache, layered with hard and soft pencil crayons, to make the illustrations for this book.
18 19 20 21 22   SCP   10 9 8 7 6 5 4 3 2 1
❖
First Edition

For Amanda and women artists of the future.

—M. M.


For M. M., for your ideas and openness.
For R. W., for yourself.

—A. H.

Leonora's parents wanted her to be like every other well-bred English girl.
But she was not.

At the age of four, Leonora started scribbling on the walls, then on paper, and soon the pictures came flooding out. . . .

She sketched the birds that peered at her
from the stained-glass windows of her mansion.
She sketched the horses she'd seen at stables. She drew
maps of make-believe planets and illustrated fables about their
native creatures. How she loved fantastic tales! Her grandma told
enchanting legends from Ireland, the land of their ancestors. The stories
took Leonora to worlds that shimmered beyond this one, and when the spirits
flew, and the gods stirred their cauldrons, and the fairies shifted shapes, something
flew and stirred and shifted inside of her.

Though she drew more fancifully and more often than most proper girls, her mother and father took little note of it. They wanted her to become a lady, then a rich man's wife. So when Leonora turned nine, they packed her off to boarding school.

But her dreaminess went with her. She could neither pay attention nor follow rules. The teachers said Leonora was unteachable and expelled her from one school, then another.

Still, at Miss Penrose's Academy in Italy, Leonora made an important discovery. On visits to churches and galleries she saw paintings that opened into forests full of knights on horseback, into glittering cities where people dressed in luscious colored garments. The art reminded her of places she'd been before, in her favorite stories. Leonora wanted to paint her own imagined worlds.

She refused to find a husband at her debutante ball and
every other fancy place her parents forced her to go. There was
only one thing she wanted: to become an artist.

An artist! In those days that was highly unsuitable, especially for ladies.
Leonora's father was horrified, and her mother was worried. "You're going to be an
old maid at twenty-five," she warned. But her parents gave in and sent her to art school.
Leonora's timing was perfect. A group of artists called surrealists was stunning London
with their mysterious creations. One of them, Max Ernst, made collages of startling sights—
a lady with a bird for a head, a creature whose body sprouted leaves. When Leonora saw his pictures,
it was like a match was struck inside her.

This was the kind of art she had to make—art that gave her strange feelings, wondrous as fairy tales! She dashed off to France, where the surrealists lived.

Leonora was barely twenty, and most of the artists there were bossy older men. Their leader, a poet dressed in bottle green, decided on the rules of the group and ran the discussions at parties and cafés. But Leonora enjoyed writing and painting alongside the surrealists. She learned to dive into her imagination, to summon memories and secret wishes. . . .

She painted a plush chair in her childhood home. A little version of her took a seat. Out flowed her hair like a wild mane. Up went her rocking horse to the ceiling. A hyena tiptoed toward her hand.

Leonora and the other female surrealists were thrilled to be making art from a woman's point of view. They had no interest in painting women who looked like pretty decorations, as men had done for centuries. Leonora was just beginning to unleash her artistic powers when a terrible thing happened.

In 1940, Germany invaded Western Europe. Nazi soldiers arrested and locked up thousands of people in France, including surrealists. Artists and writers fled the country, and so did Leonora.

Many of the refugees ended up miles and miles away in Mexico, where they were welcome.

It was hard to get used to a new home. It was hard to paint at first.

Mexico astonished Leonora—the huge exotic plants in the markets, the *curanderos* on the road selling insects, lizards, and magic herbs.

Leonora befriended a Spanish artist named Remedios, who lived in a broken-down apartment filled with cats, stones, and magic crystals.

Remedios loved the same old Italian paintings as Leonora and felt the same mystical connection to the moon and the stars and all of nature. The two women talked and laughed for hours.

They cooked up stories and weird concoctions. Remedios invented a recipe for dreaming you're the king of England. Leonora made up a magic spell to cure Remedios when she was sick.

Leonora felt safe. She felt strong. She popped a chocolate in her mouth and reached for her paintbrush. She painted a house filled with enchanted women. One of them branched into a tree, another floated through the ceiling, while others brewed a bubbling green potion.

In 1943, Leonora met a friend of Remedios's, a photographer named Chiki. The two of them fell in love and later married. But nothing kept Leonora from painting—not struggling to earn money, not tending to her husband and children.

She painted with a baby in one hand, a paintbrush in the other. She was like a wizard, stirring egg into her tempera paints, mixing cinnabar, vermilion, and golden umber.

And her women did things they didn't do in paintings made by men. Instead of lying on a couch, they were listening to the stars. Instead of posing in gowns, they were going on magical processions. They were friends with monkeys, Minotaurs, and mythic birds.

An art collector paid Leonora a visit. The studio was shabby, but in her paintings such miracles took place, in such colors, shining like jewels on the throat of queens. "Could you make more?" he asked.

Could she!

Leonora imagined a giantess, with golden wheat for hair, cradling a tiny egg. She painted her on a wooden panel, and it charmed the visitors at her first one-woman exhibition in New York City.

In the years
that followed,
Leonora's fantastic
sculptures perched on
the streets of Mexico, her
luminous sets and costumes
delighted theatergoers, and her
mystical paintings became
known throughout the world.
She made art until her skin wrinkled
and her hair turned gray.

She was never rich and never proper,
and she never moved back to England. But
she became the woman she wanted to be. For
Leonora, art was a way to love the universe and
understand it. In her paintings, women have special
gifts; they can do things beyond anybody's wildest
dreams—which is marvelous, and it's powerful, and it's true.

## Author's Note

Leonora Carrington is known for her dreamlike paintings depicting mystical women and fantastic creatures. She was influenced by surrealism, a movement of artists and writers that used strange, illogical images from the subconscious mind. Like other females in the group, Leonora explored the roles and challenges of women in society. This was a new subject for artists, who traditionally were men.

Leonora was born on April 6, 1917, in Lancashire, England, to a wealthy textile manufacturer and his wife. Inspired by the Irish tales she heard from her nanny and family, especially her grandmother, Leonora began to draw and write at an early age. Later she was sent to strict convent schools but was expelled for failing to cooperate and follow rules.

During her time at Miss Penrose's Academy of Art in Italy, Leonora had the opportunity to see many fine examples of Renaissance art. She loved the colors, the way you could see inside the rooms of the buildings, and how the paintings told stories. This would have a lasting influence on her art. When she was presented at court, Leonora made no effort to attract a rich husband. Her parents then grudgingly let her study painting in London.

While in London, Leonora became intrigued with surrealism. At a dinner party she met Max Ernst, one of the famous painters of the movement. The two of them fell in love and later lived in France, where they socialized with Pablo Picasso, André Breton, Marcel Duchamp, and other surrealist artists and writers. Although Ernst was her greatest teacher, Leonora felt a kinship with women in the group, which included Leonor Fini.

After Ernst was imprisoned during World War II, the couple drifted apart. To escape France, Leonora married Renato Leduc, a Mexican diplomat and friend of Picasso's. They lived in New York before immigrating to Mexico, and then divorced. In her adopted home, Leonora met local artists Diego Rivera and Frida Kahlo, as well as other refugees from Europe, including the photographer Emérico Weisz, whom she later married.

Of all the friends Leonora made in Mexico, Remedios Varo was the closest and dearest. The two saw each other daily for many years, sharing their love of cooking, folk tales, myth, alchemy, and mysticism.

In 1947, Edward James, a rich British art collector, arranged for Leonora's paintings to be shown at the Pierre Matisse Gallery in New York. The exhibition brought her wide recognition.

For the rest of her life, Leonora worked as a painter, sculptor, and writer. She received several commissions, had many solo exhibitions, and was in demand on both sides of the Atlantic. She died at the age of ninety-four in Mexico.

## Illustrator's Note

Michelle Markel came up with the idea for *Out of This World* after we'd had a collaborative meeting here in Cambridge, England. I had previously illustrated Michelle's picture book text for *The Fantastic Jungles of Henri Rousseau* and had found the whole experience really fulfilling. I loved Michelle's spare and powerful text, the historical research involved, and the creative challenge of depicting a real artist's life and work.

Working on *Out of This World* has given me all that and more! The journey has been an involving and fascinating one, as I have long been drawn to Leonora's enigmatic images. Because she only died so recently, the specific challenge for me was to convey the spirit, themes, and sensibility she explored in her creative output without attempting to re-create literally any of her actual imagery. Since working on *Out of This World*, I have also become familiar with aspects of her extraordinary life story and her determination to forge her own creative and personal authenticity. That was all the more remarkable in the context of such historical and global turbulence.

## Selected Bibliography

Aberth, Susan. *Leonora Carrington: Surrealism, Alchemy and Art.* London: Lund Humphries, 2004.

Carrington, Leonora. Introduction by Marina Warner. Translations by Katherine Talbot and Marina Warner. *The House of Fear: Notes from Down Below.* New York: Dutton, 1988.

Chadwick, Whitney. *Women Artists and the Surrealist Movement.* New York: Thames & Hudson, 1991.

Van Raay, Stefan, Joanna Moorhead, and Teresa Arca. *Surreal Friends: Leonora Carrington, Remedios Varo and Kati Horna.* London: Lund Humphries, 2010.

*Leonora Carrington—the Mexican Years.* San Francisco: Mexican Museum, 1991.